Other People, Other Places

KV-579-460

Acknowledgements

Grateful acknowledgement is made to the following for permission to use copyright material:

Abelard-Schuman Limited for "Great Day in Ghana" adapted from *Great Day in Ghana: Kwasi Goes to Town* by Geraldine Kaye. Copyright © 1962, by Abelard-Schuman Limited. By permission of Abelard-Schuman Limited. All rights reserved. Also for "The Skating Race" adapted from *Great Day in Holland: The Skating Race* by Rutgers van der Loeff. Copyright © 1965, by Abelard-Schuman Limited. By permission of Abelard-Schuman Limited. All rights reserved/ McIntosh and Otis, Inc. for "The Flute Player of Beppu" adapted by permission of McIntosh and Otis, Inc., from *The Flute Player of Beppu* by Kathryn Gallant, © 1960 Kathryn Gallant and Kurt Weiss/Charles Scribner's Sons for "The Sun's Travels" from *A Child's Garden of Verses* by Robert Louis Stevenson.

Every effort has been made to obtain permission for copyright material and the publishers would be grateful for any discrepancies to be notified.

Editorial consultants
James Britton/Diana Bentley/Fran Oliver/Pat Parsons/Betty Root/Anne Rogers

Level 10 artists
Don Albright/Frans Altschuler/Ray Ameijide/ Willi Baum/Mike Cassaro/Bernard D'Andrea/ Ed Emberley/Lorraine Fox/Robert Geary/Judy Sue Goodwin/George Guzzi/Tony Heald/ David Kelley/Gordon Laite/Dora Leder/Marie Michal/Jane Teiko Oka/Joan Paley/Jerry Pinkney/Albert John Pucci/Ivan Ripley/ Caroline Sharpe/Graham Smith/Lesley Smith/ Tom Ungerer/Ray Webb/Dianne Winer/Hans Zander

© Ginn and Company Ltd 1979
Ninth impression 1984   12.58406
Reading 360 Level 10 Readers set ISBN 0 602 23080 2

Published by Ginn and Company Ltd
Prebendal House, Parson's Fee, Aylesbury, Bucks HP20 2QZ

Printed in Great Britain by Ebenezer Baylis & Son Ltd
The Trinity Press, Worcester, and London

Contents

The Flute Player of Beppu

Far away in Japan is a city on the Inland Sea called Beppu. Of all the good people there, no one was so admired as the flute player. When the flute player put his flute to his lips, out came such strange, sweet music that everyone stopped to listen.

By day, the flute player wandered up into the hills above the city, along the country roads past green rice fields and neat farmers' cot-

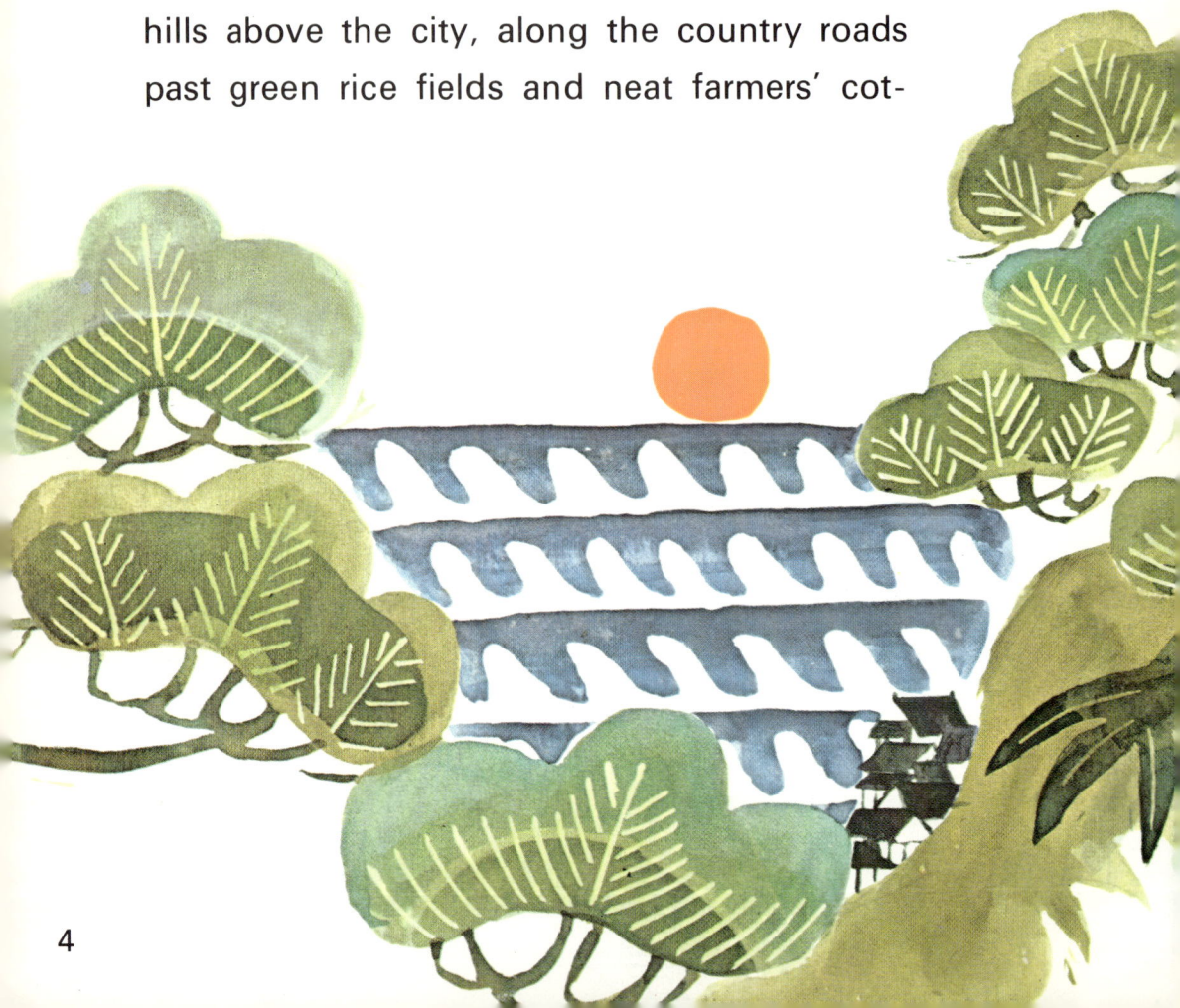

tages. Or he followed the wide roadway along the sea that led to the harbour, busy with ships loading and unloading.

At night, when Beppu was a city of a thousand lights, the flute player roamed through the narrow, winding streets. Often he stopped outside a bright teahouse.

Wherever the flute player went, people loved the music he played.

One of the many people who waited each day for the flute player was a small boy named Sato-san. Sato-san lived on his father's farm up in the green hills above the city. He knew well the country sounds — of birds, of crickets, the

songs of farmers as they planted or harvested rice. But best of all he loved the sound of the flute player's flute.

Each day Sato-san would stand by the side of the road until he heard the strange sweet music of the flute. Then, because he was shy, he would hide behind bushes, listening to the wonderful music until the flute player had gone on down the road.

One summer day Sato-san was walking along the road in front of his father's house. His wooden shoes sent small puffs of dust into the air. He stumbled and fell. And there beside him on the road he saw what looked like a long piece of bamboo. It was a flute! Gently he picked it up. His fingers covered the holes of the flute one by one.

"What a lucky boy I am," he said to himself. He put the flute to his lips and out came a pure sweet tone. He smiled. "I shall learn to play you. And you and I will travel throughout the country just like the flute player and his flute."

Sato-san put the flute inside his kimono. "No one will know about you until I can play you," he said.

Now that very morning the flute player's wife had looked out of her house with its clean floors and sliding doors. There in the garden were four new morning-glory blossoms. They looked so fresh and lovely in the morning sun that she wanted the flute player himself to see

7

them. Away she went to find him. At last she saw him talking to a farmer in the road.

"Come," she said. "My morning-glory blossoms are out for the first time. You must see them in the morning sun!"

The flute player followed his wife home. Once in the garden, the two of them sipped tea and admired the four beautiful new morning-glories.

Some time later, the flute player reached into the folds of his kimono for his flute. It was gone.

"My flute!" he cried. "Where is my flute?" He couldn't remember playing it that morning. He searched the house from floor to roof, but the flute was nowhere to be found.

He hurried out into the streets of Beppu, asking everyone, "Have you seen my flute?" Each one shook his head.

The flute player hurried down to the harbour. Three ships were in, and men were busy loading and unloading. "Have you seen my flute?" the flute player cried. The men shook their heads.

The sun was high when the flute player set out for the country lanes. At farmhouses, in the rice fields, he stopped people to ask, "Have you seen my flute?" But everyone shook his head — all but one small boy. And nobody saw *him*. For Sato-san had already scampered towards home.

By the time the flute player started sadly back to the city, the boy had rushed through the front garden and was lying on the hay in his father's barn.

Sato-san brought out the flute he had found. His eyes shone. "You are *my* flute," he said. "I will learn to play such music that everyone will stop to listen. *I* found you. You belong to me."

Then Sato-san remembered how sad the flute player had looked. What if the flute he had found belonged to the flute player?

What would the flute player do without his flute and his music? Would he wander through the streets, still looking for his flute, stopping in bright teahouses, and asking, "Have you seen my flute?"

Sato-san looked again at the flute. "I found you," he said. "I will take good care of you. I will never lose you."

But the more Sato-san looked at the flute, the more he thought of the flute player. And the more he thought, the more Sato-san knew what he must do.

He heard his mother call. Slowly he got up

and, with the flute in his hands, he walked into the yard. His mother was waiting for him.

"I shall be late for supper," he said. "There is something I must do, for I have found a flute which may belong to the flute player."

His mother threw up her hands. "What? You have found the flute player's flute?"

"Now," said Sato-san, "I must return it."

So, just as the sun moved down behind the

high hills, Sato-san started for the edge of town. He carried the flute ever so gently. By the time he reached the flute player's house, the first stars were twinkling in the evening sky. The lights of the town were beginning to go on. Sato-san pushed open the gate and called out, "Flute-player-san! Flute-player-san!"

The door slid open and there, bowing before

Sato-san, was the flute player's wife. She asked him to come in. He took off his shoes and placed them outside the door next to the shoes of the flute player and his wife. Then he stood up and said, "I think I've found the flute player's flute!"

The flute player's wife threw up her hands. "You have found the flute player's flute!" she cried. She scurried into another room, calling, "He has found the flute! the flute!" Sato-san followed her.

The flute player was sitting by a low table, chopsticks in hand, and a bowl of rice before him. He looked up, surprised and happy. "Come in," he said.

Shyly Sato-san looked at the man whom everyone loved and admired. His eyes were kind. Slowly Sato-san reached inside his kimono and brought out the flute.

"Ah," said the flute player. "My flute!" He put the flute to his lips. Out came the strange sweet music that Sato-san knew and loved so well.

The flute player's wife brought in a bowl of

steaming rice and placed it on the table. She pushed a cushion up to the table and bowed to Sato-san.

"Please sit down," she said. Sato-san sank down on the cushion. Then the flute player and Sato-san together picked up their chopsticks and began to eat.

No one spoke for a long time. At last Sato-san said, "I found the flute in the road in front of my father's farm."

"Ah, so," said the flute player.

"I didn't return it right away," said Sato-san. "I didn't know it was yours." He looked up. The flute player was watching him quietly. "I didn't want it to be yours," said Sato-san. "I wanted it for myself."

The flute player's eyes grew wide.

"I have heard your music many times. And I love it," Sato-san said. "I wanted the flute so that I could learn to play such music as you do."

The flute player set down his rice bowl. "And why do you like my music?"

"Because," said Sato-san, "it makes me think of cherry trees, pink as a sea-shell in the

spring, of green damp rice fields in the early morning, of shining ships in the harbour, and of wood smoke in the autumn."

The flute player smiled. "I was once young like you. When I heard the old flute player's music, it made me, too, think of all the things of which you speak. It was my greatest dream to be a flute player."

Sato-san said shyly, "It is mine, too."

"Then we shall see," said the flute player. "Because you are a truthful boy, and because you love the music of my flute, I shall teach you how to play it. You will come with me every day. We will go up into the hills above the city along the country roads. We will follow the wide roadway along the sea that leads to the harbour. And at night we will go through the narrow streets of the town."

"Oh!" cried Sato-san, his brown eyes shining. "When will you teach me?"

"Tomorrow morning we will begin," said the flute player.

That night, before Sato-san went to sleep, he shut his eyes and saw himself wandering with the flute player throughout the countryside. That night he dreamed that one day he would play the flute himself.

And so it happened. If you should ever travel to that far-off city and hear a flute tune — strange and sweet — you will know that you are listening to Sato-san, the boy who became the flute player of Beppu.

Kathryn Gallant

Great Day in Ghana

Kwasi cut himself a new piece of soap from the bar on the shelf, picked up his bucket and walked across the village to the tap. Several boys were already there with their buckets. They soaped themselves till they were covered with white foam from head to toe, scrubbing at their bodies with handfuls of dried grass. Kwasi had never seen them work so hard at their baths before. They wanted to be extra clean, for it was the eve of Independence Day. Tomorrow, 6th March, was a great day of celebration. It was Ghana's Independence Day.

"I am going to Accra tomorrow," said Kwasi. "I am going right to Accra on the mammy wagon to see my grandmother."

The boys looked at him with round eyes. "You might get lost. You are too small to go so far," said one of them.

"Oh, I've been before," Kwasi boasted.

"You will miss the celebrations here," said another boy. "You will miss the feasting and drumming and dancing."

"It will be better still in Accra," said Kwasi. "There will be fireworks."

"Listen," said the boys. "The drumming is starting already."

"It is Kofi," said one of the boys. "He has started already. He would drum all day and all night if he could."

"He is the best drummer in the village," said Kwasi.

"He is the best in all the villages around," said another boy.

They began to move their feet to the sound of the drumming. Blobs of soap flew this way and that, like blossoms on a windy day.

Kwasi had finished his bath. He walked back

to his house.

"Kwasi, is that you?" asked his mother. She was cooking at the fire beside the house. She had a pot of soup and a big pan of rice. Kwasi sniffed the soup hungrily.

"Come, it is time to eat," his mother called. "Here Amma, take this to your father." Amma was Kwasi's sister. She took the pot of food from her mother and went over to the men sitting under the trees. Kwasi and the rest of the children crowded round the big pot.

All this time the drumming went on. Some-

times it was fast and sometimes it was slow, but it went on and on like a great heart beating. Quite a number of people were dancing now. That was how the drumming was. It made people dance even if they didn't want to. It pulled them like a strong cord. Soon the whole village would be dancing. It pulled at the children too. They made a little group of their own just outside the circle of grown-up people, watching how they moved their feet and their bodies and trying to dance in the same way. They danced until they were tired.

It was long after dark when Kwasi crept onto

his mat and went to sleep.

When Kwasi woke it was still dark, but there was a faint glow in the sky and he knew that the sun would soon rise. He got up and washed his face. He must hurry. The mammy wagon would get to his village soon after sunrise. He chewed a bit of stick to clean his teeth. It tasted sharp and clean. The rest of the family were still asleep.

Kwasi walked across the village. The road ran along at the end of the village and, as Kwasi walked towards it, he heard the mammy wagon and he began to run. The green lorry drew up at the side of the road. Somebody let the flap down and Kwasi climbed into the lorry. It was already full of people and all of them had baskets and bundles. Kwasi managed to find a place to sit.

The lorry started off, swaying a little as it went down the road. The driver began to sing and everybody joined in. Kwasi did not know the words of the song, but he beat his feet on the floor in time to the rhythm.

At last, after the long ride, the lorry reached Accra and everybody jumped down. Kwasi walked towards his grandmother's house. The streets were full of people.

His grandmother lived in the old part of the town. She was a cake seller. She fried cakes for the people passing by to eat.

When he saw his grandmother, Kwasi began to run. "Grandmother," he called out. "Grandmother, I have come."

Kwasi's grandmother sat on her wooden stool behind her fires. She did not get up, for she hardly ever moved from her stool.

"Kwasi, my grandson," she said. "Let me look at you. You have grown a lot in a year."

"Grandmother," said Kwasi quickly, "are you coming to the celebrations?"

"I must make cakes, Kwasi. People still want

to eat on Independence Day. I am too old for singing and dancing. Such things are for young people. You go, Kwasi, and in the evening I will meet you at the Independence Arch. We will watch the fireworks together."

"But how shall I find the Independence Arch?" asked Kwasi.

"You can see it from far away. It is shaped like this," said Kwasi's grandmother. Quickly she made the arch with a piece of batter and dropped it in the hot fat to cook. When it was cooked she gave it to Kwasi.

"The arch is like this. Anyone will show you

the way. Take some more cakes. Take as many as you like.'' Some people were coming down the street, dancing as they came.

''But Grandmother . . .'' began Kwasi. Before he had time to say any more the people closed round him in a circle, pressing against him so that he had to dance with them. ''Goodbye, Grandmother,'' he called.

Kwasi looked around. There was a low wall close by and he sat down to get his breath.

''You dance well for such a small boy,'' said a voice beside him. A boy a little older than Kwasi was also sitting on the wall.

"My name is Kojo," said the boy. "I will stay with you. You might get lost by yourself."

"I won't get lost," said Kwasi, taking out his grandmother's cakes. "I won't get lost because I've got this cake to help me find my way."

"Independence Arch," cried the boy. "That's where I'm going. I will show you the way." The two boys wandered down the street, eating the rest of the cakes.

"What's that coming down the street?" asked Kwasi. "I can hear drumming."

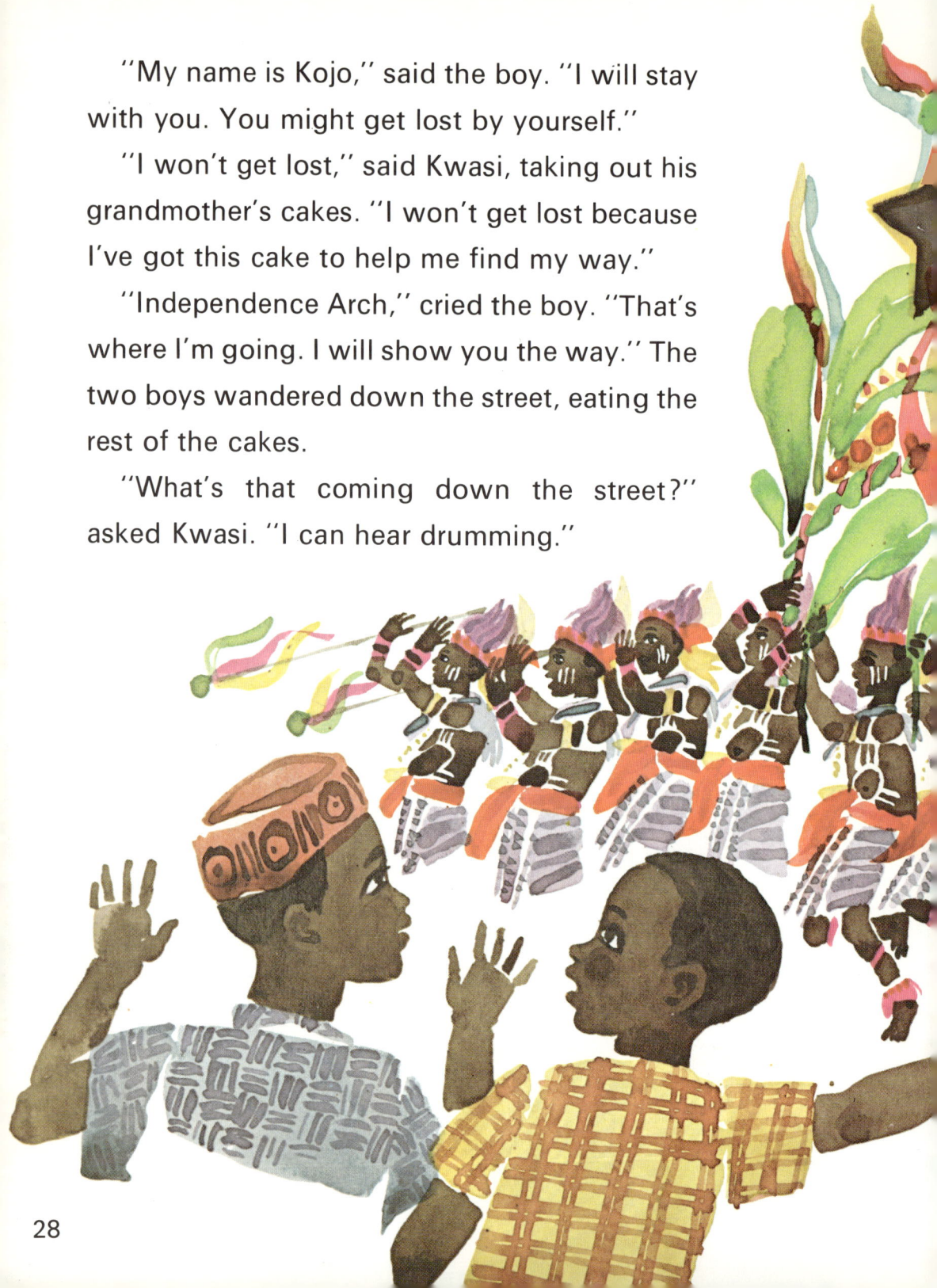

It was a parade. First came a group of dancers, their bodies painted with white patterns. Behind them was a man carrying a huge drum on his shoulders, and then another with an enormous red umbrella trimmed with gold. In the shade of the umbrella walked a chief. He was a very old chief, and he walked slowly.

"It is one of the chiefs," said Kojo. "Many chiefs are gathering here to watch the drumming and dancing."

"We won't be able to see anything," said Kwasi. "Let's climb those palm trees. Then we shall see." From the palm trees the two boys looked down upon the crowd. They looked down upon the heads of the people, and upon the huge circles of the chiefs' umbrellas — yellow and blue and red and purple. The umbrellas twirled and nodded like huge flowers.

"My arms are tired and I am thirsty," said Kwasi in a little while, "and I must get to Independence Arch before nightfall."

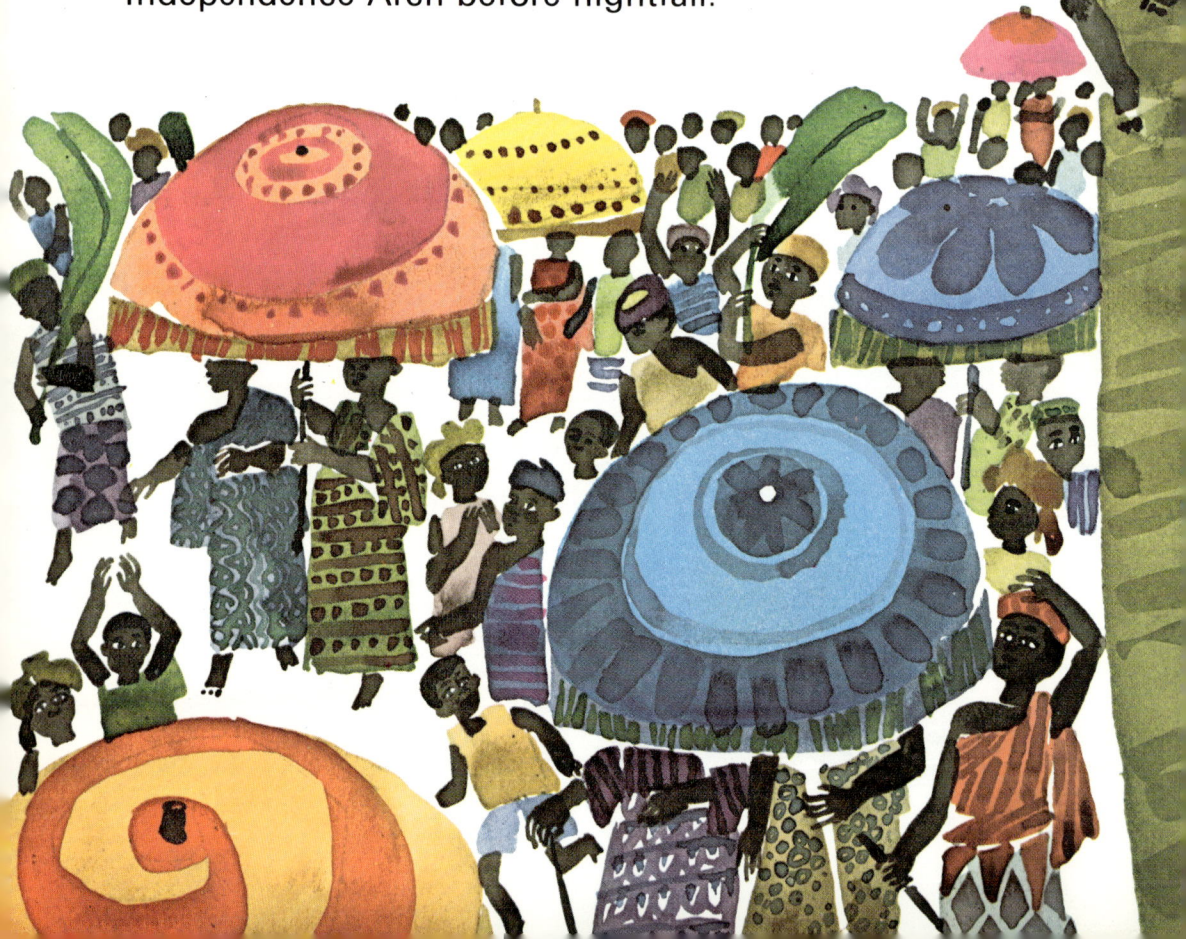

He picked a coconut and slid down the tree. The boys shared the sweet coconut milk as they walked. Finally Kojo said, "Look!"

Kwasi looked round. Ahead of him was a long grassy slope and at the top was the Independence Arch, shaped just like the cake that Grandmother had given him. Hundreds of people were gathered on the grass around the arch, waiting for the fireworks.

"Come on, Kojo, I've got to find my grandmother," called Kwasi over his shoulder. It was Grandmother who saw Kwasi first.

"Here you are, Kwasi," she said. "So you found your way. You didn't get lost. Have you seen the dancing and the drumming?"

"Oh yes," said Kwasi. "This is my new friend, Grandmother. His name is Kojo. He helped me to find my way."

Grandmother and the two boys sat on the grass. While they waited, they ate the cakes which Grandmother had brought them. The sky above them grew dark and the stars came out. A cool breeze blew in from the sea. A hush fell on the murmuring voices.

Suddenly there was a bang that made Kwasi hold his ears. A rocket shot into the sky and burst into scarlet stars. For a moment they hung in the sky, then they floated gently towards the earth.

"Is it magic?" whispered Kwasi.

"It is not magic," said his grandmother, "it is the start of the fireworks."

Kwasi stared into the sky above him. "Independence Day," he whispered. "It is a great day indeed when there are red blossoms in the night sky."

Geraldine Kaye

THE SUN'S TRAVELS

The sun is not a-bed when I
At night upon my pillow lie;
Still round the earth his way he takes,
And morning after morning makes.

While here at home, in shining day,
We round the sunny garden play,
Each little Indian sleepy-head
Is being kissed and put to bed.

And when at eve I rise from tea,
Day dawns beyond the Atlantic Sea,
And all the children in the West
Are getting up and being dressed.

Robert Louis Stevenson

The Skating Race

"Yelle, are you asleep?" whispered Bouke to his brother. There was a streak of white moonlight on the floor. Outside, everything was cold and white. But here in bed it was nice and warm.

"Did you hear the news?" whispered Bouke. "They need three horses to pull the snow-

plough. The snow has never been so thick, but the ice on the canal hasn't either."

Yelle just wanted to sleep. There had been far too much talk these last few days — talk about the snow, the ice, whether it would hold long enough. But he was as proud as the others of "their" race.

He was proud of the dangerous track which covered more than a hundred miles along the frozen canals, which went right through the "eleven old towns", across wind-swept lakes, past tiny villages and lonely farmhouses. Yet skaters must push on through the icy winter darkness. Oh, how he longed to be one of them, to be old enough! Perhaps Auke, his brother. . . .

But now that the snow was so thick, how could they possibly clear the track and make it fit for skating?

When the boys came down for breakfast, the kettle was singing on the stove and there was frost on the windows. The radio was on. There was special news about the race. Helpers would be needed to clear the track, and school children were to have a holiday so that they could help.

"Hurrah," shouted Bouke, "just give me a broom!" But Yelle sat there quietly. Auke got up and left the room without a word. Yelle followed him with his eyes. Bouke thought, "There is something the matter with Auke, and Yelle knows what it is."

A minute later Auke poked his head inside again. "I am going over to Tabe's," he said.

Tabe worked at Farmer Terpstra's, next door. He was the best skater of the village. Tabe was big and strong and very fast. But Auke had a better style. They skated a lot together, but only Tabe went in for races. He had won seven medals already. But he hadn't got the Eleven Towns Cross yet. Would he this year? Everybody knew he had put his name down for the race.

The winner of the Eleven Towns Cross is a hero. At school the picture of the last winner hung just under the picture of the Queen. Fancy, thought Bouke, our Tabe hanging underneath the Queen!

The boys pulled on warm coats and pulled their caps down over their ears. As they went outside, Yelle swung the snow shovel over his shoulder and Bouke picked up a broom. They walked down the snowy path. It was bitterly cold. The breath came out of their mouths in little white clouds. They headed for the canal.

That evening Bouke was more quiet. He was tired from sweeping away all that snow, and he was unhappy about Yelle. It was just as if Yelle was hiding something and it made him very quiet. Mother was quiet too. She asked about Auke only once.

"Auke is helping Farmer Terpstra now because Tabe is away," Bouke answered. "He will stay there tonight and all day tomorrow."

Yelle turned on the radio for the news. "From all over the country skaters have come to the Eleven Towns Race: two hundred and seven for the race, more than five thousand to skate along after them. The town of Leeuwarden, where they will start before daybreak, is now filled. No more rooms are to be had, and many people will have to sit up all night. All racers must be checked by a doctor. The bodies of the racers must be well protected against the cold. Cream on the face. . . ."

"Bedtime," said Father. "It will be an early start tomorrow."

The alarm clock rattled. It must be early morning, but it was still pitch black. In a flash,

Yelle remembered: they are off, the skaters . . . in the dark . . . finding their way across the ice with torches, stumbling over ice that sticks up in some places, falling into the cracks they can't see! The first few hours are the hardest, he knew, when the skaters try to pass each other, all black shadows in a hurry, when they fall and others pile up on top of them.

After milking, when Yelle went outside, the icy wind almost stopped his breath. Then he saw the sun rising and he felt better. Soon the skaters would be able to see.

After the children had finished their chores, Father asked them, "Shall we drive to the vil-

lage, to see if there is any news yet?" The boys scrambled into the front seat of the truck beside Father.

The village was all astir. The streets were crowded with people. "When will the first skaters be here?" asked Father.

"Not before eleven," said the head of the village skating club. He was one of the six men who would later sit at the checking point. They would stamp the cards which showed what time each skater had arrived.

Yelle went onto the canal. Suddenly he heard cheering.

"Tabe has almost caught up with the leading group," he heard. "But there is somebody else with him — no one knows who."

Someone turned to ask Yelle, "I haven't seen your Auke all day. Isn't he with you?"

Yelle felt himself getting red in the face. He hurried away, pretending that he hadn't heard.

"There they are," yelled a boy.

There was loud cheering everywhere. The men behind the checking table were ready. The first skaters could be seen. Yelle stared at the men who came whizzing by, bent almost double. They braked and shot towards the checking table, where they held out their cards to be stamped. Everybody was shouting: "Keep it up! You're doing fine! We're proud of you!"

And Tabe, where was Tabe? There – the last one, but then, this *was* the leading group. Tabe got a special cheer. He was their man.

The whole village was thrilled to think that their Tabe might be the winner! There he was off again, after drinking a cup of hot milk and egg. He was no longer the last one. He caught up with numbers seven and eight, then passed them. Soon the group was out of sight.

Yelle's heart sank. He was the only one who had been watching for that other skater who should have been with Tabe and wasn't. Then he heard, "The next group is coming!"

Dare he look? Yes, there in the middle of the second group was the one he was looking for — a quiet, slim skater with a cap pulled down over his head.

All of a sudden someone shouted, "But that's Auke!" At once hundreds of people were calling his name. Yelle could not join in, there was such a lump in his throat.

"Didn't you know?" someone shouted at him. "Didn't you know that Auke was in the race?" Auke was cheered almost as much as Tabe. Tabe was a giant among skaters. But they were proud of Auke too.

Auke was off again. He was less hurried than the others, but just as fast. Everyone shouted after him. Yelle wanted to shout too, but he couldn't. He had lost his voice. His eyes smarted

with tears. Yelle saw Auke speeding away. Auke hadn't even seen him.

Suddenly Yelle felt an arm round his shoulder. It was Father. "You knew it, didn't you?" Father asked.

Yelle nodded, he still could not speak. There was something in Father's voice that made him feel very happy. "It is the greatest surprise of my life," Father said.

Bouke came running towards Yelle, his face as red as a beetroot. Now Yelle was pleased to see him. He did not want to hide from people any more.

Suddenly the news spread like wildfire: the leading group is nearing Leeuwarden, the finishing point, and only five of them are left. Their names are given, but Tabe's is not among them. Their Tabe had given up! But an un-known skater has pulled ahead ·from the second group. Can it be Auke?

"Come along," said Father. "We can watch the finish on television at Farmer Terpstra's."

In Farmer Terpstra's living room the family is sitting on the floor in front of the television set.

There is the finishing line on the screen. And there in a flash are the skaters. You can't see who they are . . . they're too close together.

There, they're drawing apart . . . that third one, can it be Auke? People are cheering and stamping in the snow. Number three passes number two. Yelle's heart nearly bursts.

It *is* Auke, you can tell by the way he skates. Yelle sees Auke come even with number one. There is a roar from the crowd. The unknown skater whizzes past the finish. And then they

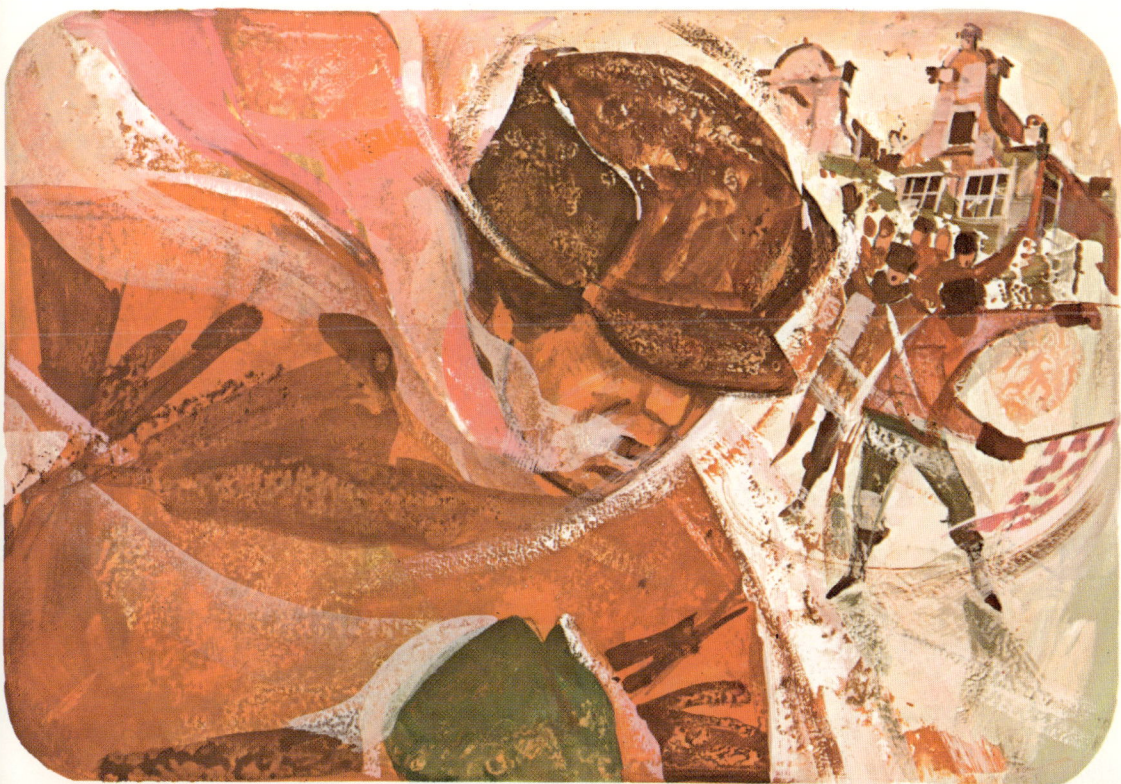

hear the winner's name, and the name of their village.

Auke is lifted shoulder high, then suddenly his face appears, filling the screen. His sweater, his cap, his eyebrows, everything is white with frost. He is still breathing hard. "I am happy," he says.

Yelle felt Father's arm round his shoulder, squeezing it. But of course it was Bouke who found the breath to shout, "Now our Auke's picture will hang underneath the Queen's!"

Rutgers van der Loeff

Glossary

admire   to look at or think about with wonder, pleasure and approval

arch   *1* curved or rounded part of building or bridge *2* monument in this shape

astir   moving about; in motion; also, out of bed; up

bamboo   tree-like grass that grows in warm regions. The strong hollow stems are used for canes, furniture and sometimes for houses

batter   *1* to beat with repeated blows   *2* thin mixture made up of flour, milk, eggs, used to make foods, e.g. biscuits and cakes

boast   to speak too well of oneself

celebration   activities or special services in honour of somebody or something

chopsticks   small sticks of wood or ivory used in pairs to carry food to the mouth

dare   *1* to be bold enough *2* to challenge

draw apart   to pull away

eve   day before an important event

head   *1* part of body containing the brain   *2* to move towards   *3* chief person; leader

hero   brave man or boy

independence   freedom from the control, influence or help of others

kimono   loose outer garment, held in place with a sash, worn by both men and women in Japan

mammy wagon   type of truck fitted out as a bus for people and to carry farm produce and farm animals, such as chickens

murmur   low muttering sound

pitch   dark sticky substance

rhythm   regular beat

roam   to wander or ramble

scamper   to run lightly and quickly

scurry   to run in a quick and hurried way

smart   *1* to feel sharp pain *2* bright or fresh in appearance *3* clever

stumble   to miss one's footing and lurch forward

style   manner or fashion

tone   *1* quality of a sound *2* tint or shade

trim *1* neat, well kept
2 to decorate around edge

twirl to turn round rapidly; to spin; to whirl

wander to stroll from place to place